RAIDERS OF THE LOST BARK

Illustrated by: Carl G. Moore

Dog Debates

3.

Dog Practical Jokes

5.

Dog Cooking Shows

For a while, Spot was content to beg at the table.
Then, one day, without warning...

7.

Dog Analysis

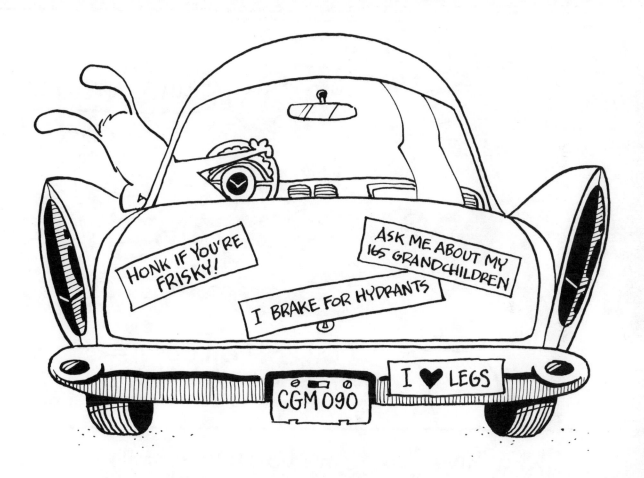

Why There Aren't Any Dog Restaurants

Pekingese Protests

Fifi Describes Her Blind Date

13.

Every Day
Pierre Went
to the
Same Place
to Go to
the Bathroom

Bosco Joins a Support Group
for Suckers of the Fake-the-Throw Gag

15.

Lady MacBeth's Dog Chews Her Slippers
One Too Many Times

16.

As the Result of a Misunderstanding, Ruff Fetches a Hick

17.

Rex Discovers That He Is, Indeed, Barking Up the Wrong Tree

18.

19.

How the Bulldog Got Its Name

Professor Davis Always Uses a Pointer

21.

The Not-So-Great Dane

Another Sheepdog's Career Ruined
By Too Much Thinking

With His Owners on Vacation,
Spike Turns Entrepreneur

Dog Aerobics

Shih Tzu Feeding Times

Why Dogs Shouldn't Become Orthopedic Surgeons

28.

Four-Star Hotels for Dogs

29.

30.

Dog Bosses

Why Dogs Make Lousy Firemen

Why Dog Surprise Parties Don't Work

33.

34.

Dog Mirages

35.

Madge Learned the Hard Way Not to Wear
Her Bunny Slippers Jogging

Dog Romances

38.

One Thing Seemed Certain. Spotty Would Never Be Asked
to Serve As Entertainment Chairperson Again

40.

Dog Detectives

42.

Dog Attorneys

43.

Moms of the Dog World

45.

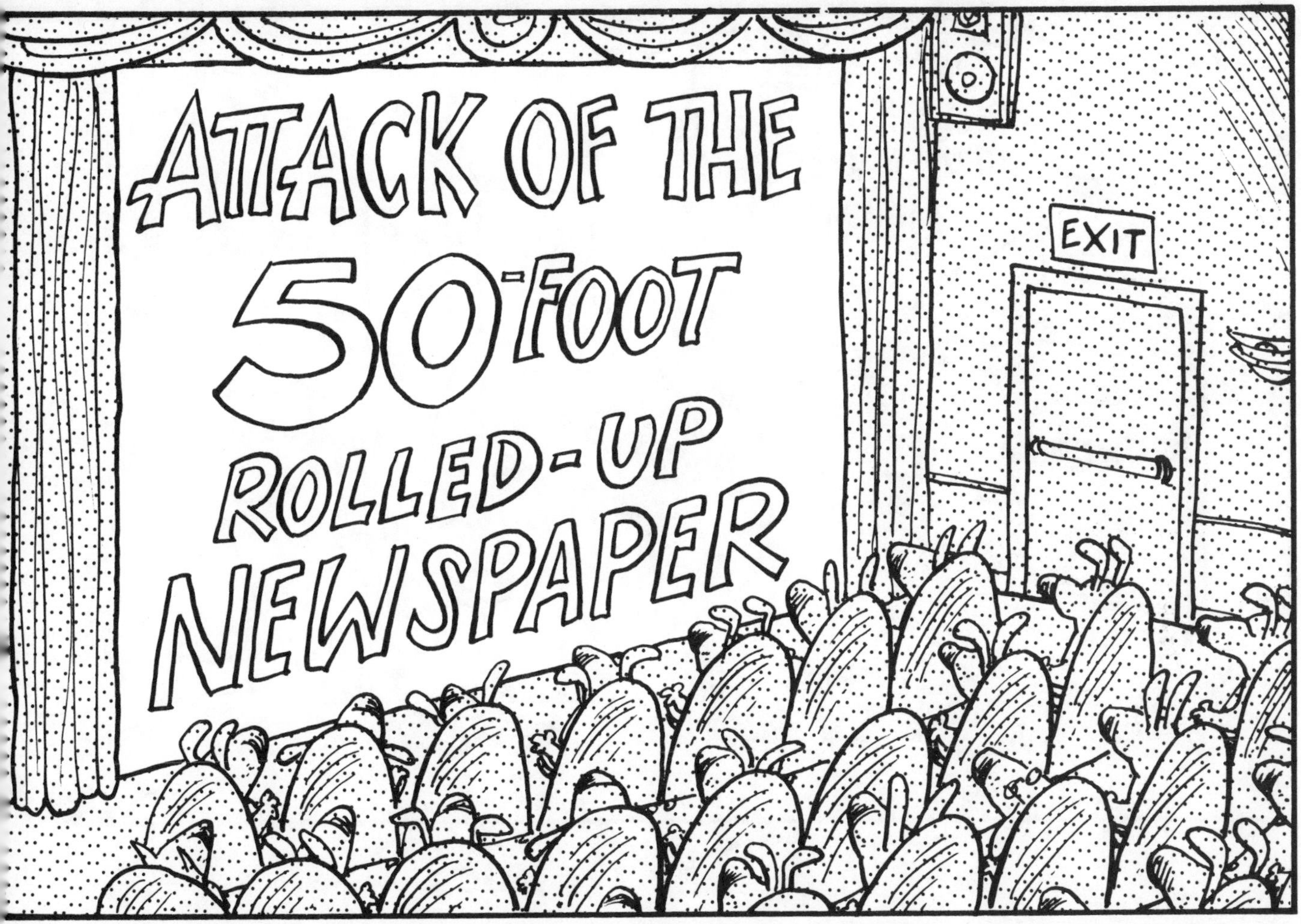
ATTACK OF THE
50-FOOT
ROLLED-UP
NEWSPAPER
EXIT

Dog Peer Pressure

48.

Scotty Considered Himself a Scratch Golfer

51.

Dog Commencement Speeches

Pepper Has an Attitude Problem

53.

54.

When Dogs Dine Out

Lassie: The Later Years

Dog Nightmares

The Indianapolis 500 for Dogs

59.

Dog Rock Concerts

Riot at the Dog Prison

Weredogs

Why Dogs Make Lousy Baseball Players

Sparky's First Flight

67.

Famous Dog Monuments

70.

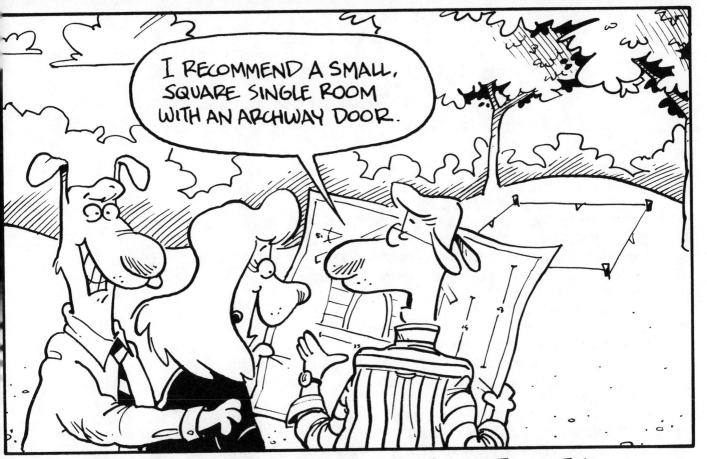

Why Dog Architects Have Such an Easy Job

Other books from

SHOEBOX GREETINGS
(A tiny little division of Hallmark)

HEY GUY, ARE YOU: A) Getting Older? B) Getting Better? C) Getting Balder?

FRISKY BUSINESS: All About Being Owned by a Cat.

THE WORLD ACCORDING TO DENISE.

GIRLS JUST WANNA HAVE FACE LIFTS: The Ugly Truth About Getting Older.

DON'T WORRY, BE CRABBY: Maxine's Guide to Life.

EVERYTHING YOU ALWAYS WANTED TO KNOW ABOUT STRESS...but were too nervous, tense, irritable and moody to ask.

40: THE YEAR OF NAPPING DANGEROUSLY.

THE MOM DICTIONARY.

THE DAD DICTIONARY.

WAKE UP AND SMELL THE FORMULA: The A to No ZZZZ's of Having a Baby.

WORKIN' NOON TO FIVE: The Official Workplace Quizbook.

THE OFFICIAL COLLEGE QUIZ BOOK.

WHAT...ME, 30?

STILL MARRIED AFTER ALL THESE YEARS.

YOU EXPECT ME TO SWALLOW THAT?: The Official Hospital Quiz Book.

THE GOOD, THE PLAID, AND THE BOGEY: A Glossary of Golfing Terms.

THE COLLEGE DICTIONARY: A Book You'll Actually Read!

THE FISHING DICTIONARY: Everything You'll Say About the One That Got Away.